John Retalla

HANNAH AND HANNA
IN DREAMLAND

OBERON BOOKS
LONDON

WWW.OBERONBOOKS.COM

First published in 2018 by Oberon Books Ltd
521 Caledonian Road, London N7 9RH
Tel: +44 (0) 20 7607 3637 / Fax: +44 (0) 20 7607 3629
e-mail: info@oberonbooks.com
www.oberonbooks.com

PB ISBN: 9781786826435
E ISBN: 9781786826428

Printed on FSC accredited paper

10 9 8 7 6 5 4 3 2 1

For my wife, Nina

Introduction

Since writing *Hannah and Hanna* in 2001 and having seen it performed all round the world, I thought that the play, and that particular chapter of my life, was over.

The summer of 2015, and the news of borders going up all over Europe to refugees, changed that. Jan Ryan, the tour producer of *Hannah and Hanna* in 2001-2004, suggested a second part and I've been at this task since the beginning of 2016.

Part 1 of *Hannah and Hanna in Dreamland* takes place in 1999-2000 and is a slightly edited version of the 'old' *Hannah and Hanna*. The girls are sixteen years old at the time that a large number of Kosovan refugees are welcomed by Britain. Most of them were housed in towns like Margate or in cities like Glasgow. This was Tony Blair's 'good invasion' – after Western Europe had failed to help the people of Bosnia in the conflict with Serbia, he acted swiftly to prevent the same genocide occurring in Kosovo. He was supported by U.S. President Bill Clinton. If you go to Pristina, the capital of Kosovo, today, you will see an enormous statue of Bill Clinton and a main artery of the city named Boulevard Tony Blair. As a result of the UK/US intervention, countless lives were saved, and Kosovo declared itself an independent state in 2008.

At the time, I wrote the following introduction to the play:

"I wrote *Hannah and Hanna* because I wanted to hear something for the hosts as well as the guests.

Teenagers in schools in Britain are told very little about why large groups of people from another country arrive overnight. All they know is that they are asylum-seekers, people from nowhere. National and local community leaders show an almost chronic lack of interest in 'introducing' these strangers to the local community. In school classrooms, pupils will sometimes not know where the boy or girl in the next desk is actually from.

In small towns, the reaction to asylum-seekers can be more violent, not less.

In Margate, in 1999, there was an overnight arrival of hundreds of Kosovans. The town could talk of little else; pensioners were outraged, teenagers declared war, the local newspapers had a story that would run and run.

How could a local Margate teenager – in that climate – ever meet, let alone *befriend*, a Kosovan teenager who'd survived the invasion of her country and ended up in Margate? And at what point, supposing that a friendship did develop, would the two open up to each other? Are there any circumstances which would bring about a real and unprompted exchange between them?"

Hannah and Hanna caught on; it played on and off over a five-year period in Britain and was translated into several languages.

Part 2 of *Hannah and Hanna in Dreamland* takes place in 2015. The girls are now women of thirty-two. They have, for various reasons, had almost no contact since they parted company on the road to Kosovo, near the burnt-out bus where Hanna was raped before she came to England.

By 2015, there are sixty-five million refugees on the move across the world. Migration has become the biggest challenge facing Europe. The largest group by nationality to take the perilous sea routes from North Africa or Turkey are Syrians. The war in Syria has caused a massive exodus of people from that country. The story behind every individual Syrian fleeing their country is a heart-breaking one. If we were in their shoes, we would do as they do, we'd stuff a suitcase and get out with our family while we were still alive, go anywhere that would take us.

The Syrians join people fleeing from Iraq, Pakistan, Somalia, Eritrea, Sudan, Nigeria, Afghanistan and elsewhere. In 2000 less than 100,000 people a year were claiming asylum in Europe. By 2015, the number had grown to one million.*

The increase in numbers has led to a universal hardening of attitudes towards the sheer chaos and distress that people witness in those who have lost everything. It's as if we just don't want to be affected by that level of loss and misery. It's so horribly insoluble and distressing. There is no Western country that votes for a leader who adopts a sympathetic and open-arms approach to refugees. It's all too much to contemplate and absorb: dead toddlers, thousands drowning at sea, people freezing to death in refrigerated lorries to get to Britain – no one knows what to do, no one knows how to respond.

Today the successful political leader shows a hard heart.

Yet there are many citizens who express themselves through individual and collective acts of kindness to migrants. I spent a month in Calais in the spring of 2015 and I was astonished by the energy and purpose shown by a number of retired middle-class French people who committed all their time to helping people stuck in the Jungle and unable to smuggle themselves into England. They were outdoors all day in the incredibly high winds that swept over the dunes, ferrying wood and plastic sheeting, generators for phone chargers, supplying hundreds of meals, doing whatever they could to make life bearable for the thousands trying to stow away to Dover.

It's much harder for adults than it is for teenagers to change their ways, their habits and their views; to really put themselves out. I found these pensioners inspiring. They had changed their view of retirement completely because they felt that they had to act on behalf of the migrants. It's this extraordinary change in attitude that made me ask if someone like Margate Hannah could change.

Of course, I've had to ask myself the same questions too and am disappointed to find that I am as resistant to having my life disturbed as Hannah is. But she gains so much inspiration and life from Hanna that she surrenders to her own better feelings and lets her world be turned upside down.

Her heart is not as hard as she believed it to be.

John Retallack
September, 2018

*(Note; statistics drawn from *Lights in the Distance* by Daniel Trilling, Picador 2018)

Performance history of *Hannah and Hanna*

Hannah and Hanna was first performed at the Channel Theatre Company Studio in Margate on June 21, 2001 by Alyson Coote as Margate Hannah and Celia Meiras as Kosovan Hanna.

This cast performed the play over a hundred times at venues in Edinburgh and London. They also toured London schools (with an award from the Network for Social Change) for a further three weeks.

The play won a Glasgow Herald Angel at the Edinburgh Fringe, was part of the Time Out Critics Choice festival, was nominated as Best Young People's Show at the TMA awards and also for a Race in the Media Award as a result of its broadcast on the World Service in June 2002.

In 2002-2004, UK Arts International produced the play on two national tours and three British Council tours to India, The Philippines and Malaysia.

Hannah and Hanna has been translated and performed in Hebrew, Swedish, French, Dutch, Portuguese, German and Japanese. The Swedish translation played over 250 times and the production at Theatre de Poche in Brussels over 100 times.

Hannah and Hanna is published by Oberon in *Company of Angels: 4 plays* by John Retallack.

The income from the tours of *Hannah and Hanna* launched the new writing company COMPANY OF ANGELS (2000-2016) and the subsequent commissioning of numerous plays for young people, both from the UK and continental Europe.

Thanks

In Pristina, thanks to Jeton Naziraj, Ardiana Shala and Nita Qena.

In Calais, thanks to the Odyssey Programme and its director Guy Fontaine for the bursary that allowed me to spend a month in and around the Jungle in Calais in April 2015; also to Alexia Noyon at Le Charteuse de Neuville for putting me in touch with French volunteers who worked in the camp especially Francois and Maya at L'Auberge des Migrants and Renaud. And to Tarek, Mohamed and Ahmed for talking so openly to me.

In Margate, thanks to Turner Contemporary and Theatre Royal Margate for hosting readings. Thanks also to Anna Symes, Laura Provins of Dreamland, Pam Hardiman, the Winter Gardens group and everyone else who contributed to the process.

Above all, thanks to Jan Ryan without whom this play and this project would never have happened. She is a tireless fund-raiser and both a patient and an inspirational producer. She is also a fantastic individual to work with and I count myself very lucky to have her as the driver behind this project.

Finally, thanks to all the Hannahs and Hannas who have played their parts in the ongoing life of this play – and especially to Celia Meiras, who has played every incarnation of Kosovan Hanna from 2001 to 2018.

Cast
KOSOVO HANNA   Celia Meiras
MARGATE HANNAH   Lisa Payne

Creative team
Director   John Retallack
Movement Director   Sally Marie
Designer   Rachael A Smith
Music Director   Karl James
Sound Design   Dan Scott
Lighting Design   Peter Harrison
Video & Projections   Nathan Jones
Dramaturg   Stephen Wrentmore
Literary Associate   James Baldwin

Production team
Producer   Jan Ryan
Production Manager   Darryn de la Soul
Technical Stage Manager   Alex Jolly
Marketing Manager   Francesca Baker
Audience Engagement Coordinator   Jodie Nesling
Workshop Leaders   Nathan Jones, Lisa Payne
Design Assistant   Mollie Cheek
Resource Pack   Daniel Burdsey
Graphic Design   Emma Price
                                     www.tinymaster.co.uk
Set Construction   Adam Witts

Hannah and Hanna in Dreamland is produced by UK Arts
International, Lighthouse, Poole's Centre for the Arts and The
Marlowe Canterbury in association with Theatre Royal Margate,
Folkestone Quarterhouse and Looping the Loop.

The development of *Hannah and Hanna in Dreamland* has been
supported by Arts Council England, House, Thanet District
Council and The Marlowe Roar programme. The 2018 production
is supported by Arts Council England and Kent County Council.

CELIA MEIRAS – Hanna

Celia Meiras is excited to be rediscovering the character of Hanna and finding out so many new things about her. She first played the role in 2001 in John Retallack's earlier play, at various venues including the Gilded Balloon, Edinburgh, The Arcola Theatre and BAC. She has worked at a number of theatres including The Bristol Old Vic, Soho Theatre, Lyric Theatre in Hammersmith, Young Vic and Nottingham Playhouse. She is particularly passionate about new writing and physical theatre. She has also worked in radio, television and film. Fans of *Nathan Barley* will know her as Djave Bikinus and learners of Spanish will know her as Ana in *extr@*.

LISA PAYNE – Hannah

Lisa's theatre credits include Theatre Nomad's *Uncle Vanya, La Pucelle* and *Twelfth Night*. She has also co-written and toured several original productions including *The Second Oldest Profession, A Glimpse of Stocking* and is currently working on a series of Shakespeare inspired one woman shows. Her film credits include *Ruby Blue* with Bob Hoskins and *Gypo* with Rula Lenska and Pauline McLynn. She is an experienced role play trainer and runs her own theatre in education company providing interactive plays and workshops.

JOHN RETALLACK – Writer & Director

John has written over twenty plays and adaptations for theatre and for radio. Amongst other nominations and awards, he has won three TMA/SWET awards, two Herald Angels and one Fringe First. In addition to *Hannah and Hanna in Dreamland*, his adaptation of J.B. Priestley's classic novel *The Good Companions* for Radio 4 was broadcast in March 2018, and will be repeated in 2019. He recently directed *Unicorns, Almost*, Owen Sheers' play about the poet Keith Douglas, for the Hay Festival in May 2018 and received outstanding local and national reviews for his production.

His twelve original theatre plays include *Wild Girl* (2014, Bristol Old Vic), *Truant* (2013, National Theatre of Scotland), *Arlo* (2010, Southwark Playhouse), *Risk* (2007, Tron Theatre, Glasgow), *Virgins* (2006, Edinburgh Festival and National Tour), *Sweetpeter* (2004, Polka Theatre/National Tour), *Ballroom* (2004, Riverside Studios/National Tour), and *Hannah and Hanna* (2001, National and British Council tours). He also adapted and directed *Apples* by Richard Milward (2006), *The Plague* by Camus (2000), and *Junk* by Melvyn Burgess (1998).

John was the founding Artistic Director of ATC London (1978-85) and of Company of Angels (2001-2011). He was also Artistic Director of Oldham Coliseum (1985-1988) and Oxford Stage Company (1989-1999) where he directed a dozen Shakespeare productions to wide critical acclaim. John now runs his own playwriting course in Oxford.

www.oxfordplaywriting.co.uk

SALLY MARIE – Movement Director

Sally Marie trained at Central School of Ballet, working with various companies and choreographers, including Protein Dance, Jasmin Vardimon and Tilted Productions and was nominated five times for Best Female Performance by Dance Europe and The National Dance Awards, including a spotlight award for new talent.

As a movement director, she has worked on *Nerve* at The Baron's Court Theatre, *Reasons to be Cheerful* by GRAEAE for Theatre Royal Stratford East, *The Eradication of Schizophrenia in Western Lapland* by Ridiculussmuss, and *Archipelago* for The Lighthouse Poole. Other commissions include *The Looking Boy* and *2Red* for Ignition Festival, *Cherry Pops and Frozen Snow* for Edge Hill University, *Ice Dust Chronicle* for Images and *W O N D E R L A N D* for Northern School of Contemporary Dance. She has made two solos, the first of which was performed at The Royal Opera House and five full-length works for her own company Sweetshop Revolution, winning the Mathew Bourne Award 2013, The Children's Award 2014 from Sadler's Wells and The Place, as well as nominations for Best Dance Production 2015 by The Welsh Theatre Awards and Best Independent Company 2016 by the National Dance Awards.

RACHAEL A SMITH – Designer

Rachael began designing for theatre at Battersea Arts Centre. Working alongside outstanding contemporary theatre companies and artists she learnt about the process of theatre-making and devising through play and experimentation. As associate designer at the Marlowe, her work includes *Stacked* and *The Monstrum* (NT Connections), chosen to perform at the National Theatre. With *Coney*, a BAFTA award-winning company of interactive theatre-makers, she co-created and co-designed theatrical adventures at the National Theatre, Science Museum, BAC, Whitechapel Gallery, Latitude Festival, Edinburgh Festival and internationally. With *Unclaimed Creatures* she created site-responsive live art installations and immersive encounters at the Old Vic Tunnels, Roundhouse and British Museum. Other designs include *Tangent* (New Diorama), *In Eldersfield* (Barbican Pit), *Faces in the Window* (Arcola), *Bernada Alba* (Blackheath Halls), *Bedbound* (Lion and Unicorn), *Iago* (Edinburgh – winner of Outstanding Theatre Award) and costume design for Punchdrunk Enrichment's *Against Captain's Orders* and *St Ethelberga's Hallowtide Fair*. She gained an MA in Professional Theatre Design at Bristol Old Vic Theatre School.

KARL JAMES – Music Director

Karl has worked with John Retallack on a number of plays and productions, notably as composer on *Romeo and Juliet, Comedy of Errors, Pericles, Hamlet, Johnnie Blue, Mirad, A Boy From Bosnia* and *Hannah and Hanna.* As a director Karl works with Tim Crouch and has co-directed *My Arm, An Oak Tree, ENGLAND, The Author, What Happens To Hope At The End of The Evening* and *Adler & Gibb.* Most of Karl's time is spent as director of *The Dialogue Project,* where he helps people have conversations when the stakes are high.

Audio work is Karl's passion and he is best known for his own series of podcasts *2+2=5* and *A Different Kind of Justice* for BBC Radio 4. Karl's audio work has been featured on BBC's radio series Short Cuts, Latitude Festival and in Third Coast's Filmless Festival in Chicago.

DAN SCOTT – Sound Design

Dan Scott is an artist, musician and sound designer based in Margate, Kent. He works across music, sound, listening, installation and filmmaking. In recent years he has exhibited work, and initiated and run projects at Tate Modern, Tate Britain, De La Warr Pavilion, and Battersea Arts Centre.

Dan has recently completed a PhD at the University of the Arts on listening as an artistic practice, and has a strong thread of social-engagement within his practice.

Recent projects include sound design for *Speak What You Find* (with Magic Me), a promenade theatre piece, devised with residents of Tower Hamlets, *Conference (after attar),* a collaboration with artist Caroline Bergvall for Whitstable Biennale, and *This Is Our Garden In The Morning,* written and produced by Dan for Tate Britain. He is also a tutor on MA Scenography at the Royal Central School of Speech and Drama.

PETER HARRISON – Lighting Design

Peter trained at RADA.

Recent lighting designs have included *One Hand Tied Behind Us* (Old Vic, London), *Macbeth* (Stafford Festival Shakespeare), *Rasheeda Speaking* (Trafalgar Studios), *The Canterville Ghost*, and *Wilde Creatures* (Tall Stories), *Romeo and Juliet* and *Julius Caesar* (Guildford Shakespeare Company), *Dear Brutus* and *The Cardinal* (Southwark Playhouse), and *Child of the Divide* (Polka Theatre, London/Harbourfront Centre Toronto).

Other lighting designs include *Pink Mist* (Bristol Old Vic/Bush Theatre), *Translunar Paradise* (Theatre Ad Infinitum), *Britten in Brooklyn* (Wiltons Music Hall), *The Doubtful Guest* (Hoipolloi), *Orestes* (Shared Experience), and numerous pantomimes at The Marlowe Theatre in Canterbury.

His opera and dance credits include *Paul Bunyan* (Welsh National Youth Opera), *Opera Works* (ENO Baylis), *In Nocentes* and *Home Turf* (Sadlers Wells), and *Jean and Antonin* (Gartnerplatz Theatre, Munich).

His work as an Associate lighting designer includes *Collaborators* and *As You Like It* (National Theatre), *Made in Dagenham* (Adelphi Theatre), and *The Commitments* (Palace Theatre, London).

NATHAN JONES – Video & Projections

An innovative digital artist, Nathan Jones (AKA Soopanatural) has worked as Video Designer on *Khandan*, a Birmingham Rep/Royal Court Theatre co-production, the Hip Hop Shakespeare Company's *Richard II*, and *The Legend Of Mike Smith,* created by Soweto Kinch and Jonzi D.

Other artistic collaborations include working with Iapetus Records (Yugen Blakrok tour, Fifi the RaiBlaster's *BlackMatter* exhibition), Akala, Charlie Dark, Mark De Clive-Lowe and Boy Blue Entertainment. Nathan's work has featured on BBC interactive, at London's Queen Elizabeth Hall and Royal Festival Hall, Tate Britain, Turner Contemporary, XOYO, Rome Coliseum and numerous theatre venues, music festivals and clubs in Europe and South Africa.

STEPHEN WRENTMORE – Dramaturg

Stephen Wrentmore is a British theatre director, writer, academic, and change consultant. He is currently lecturer in theatre at University of Kentucky. He was Artistic Producer at Lighthouse, Poole's Centre for the Arts until summer 2018. Formally, he was Associate Artistic Director of Arizona Theatre Company, Artistic Director of the Byre Theatre in St Andrews, and has worked at The National Theatre in London, Tate Gallery, and internationally as a director from Siberia to San Francisco.

JAN RYAN – Producer

Jan Ryan began working in theatre in 1979, first at the Tramshed in Woolwich, then InterAction, the Half Moon and Women's Theatre Group. She set up and headed the Touring Department at Birmingham Rep before establishing UK Arts International in 1992. Now based in Margate, she is committed to supporting and promoting local artists, and producing work that is relevant to the region.

DARRYN DE LA SOUL – Production Manager

Darryn de la Soul has been in the Live Events industry for the last two decades, having started out as a sound engineer. More recently she has been working as a Production Manager for various events and theatre productions, and has her own company Soulsound (www.soulsound.co.uk) which supports sound engineers in their careers.

ALEX JOLLY – Technical Stage Manager

Alex Jolly travelled from Huddersfield to Margate for a summer holiday and never made it back. During the past ten years he has worked with many artists in the UK and abroad, from Disney's stage productions in the Americas to UK theatre tours. His current roles include technical manager at the Astor Community Theatre in Deal and Audio 1 at the Dreamland amusement park in Margate.

FRANCESCA BAKER – Marketing Manager

Francesca Baker is a freelancer marketer, writer and communications specialist. She works across the arts, charity, health and consumer sectors, supporting organisations to connect with audiences. Experience includes journalism, PR, marketing and events management. Follow her on Twitter, Facebook, Instagram and her website @andsoshethinks

JODIE NESLING – Local Engagement Specialist Mentor

Jodie Nesling is an award-winning freelance journalist and arts PR professional with extensive experience in regional and national media. As Marketing Manager for POW! – Thanet's women's festival, and a PR specialist for a range of community-focused arts projects, she has a comprehensive understanding of engaging with diverse audiences, especially within east Kent.

MOLLIE CHEEK – Design Assistant

Mollie is a designer and glass artist from Broadstairs, Kent. She is currently working as a set designer for the Looping the Loop arts festival. She is also designing Dangerous Corner at the Sarah Thorne theatre. Her Instagram is @molliecheekdesigns

DANIEL BURDSEY – Resource Pack

Dr. Daniel Burdsey is a sociologist at the University of Brighton. He researches the relationship between race, ethnicity and popular culture, primarily how these structures and relations are played out in social spaces. For the last decade his work has concentrated on the English seaside. He is the author/editor of six books, including *Race, Place and the Seaside: Postcards from the Edge* (Palgrave Macmillan, 2016).

uk arts
INTERNATIONAL

UK Arts International has presented more than fifty productions in the UK and internationally, including tours of John Retallack's earlier play, *Hannah and Hanna*. UK Arts focuses on work that is culturally diverse, engages with new audiences and deals with topics that are of contemporary relevance. Previous work includes *The Harder They Come* (Barbican, Stratford East, West End, national tour, US and Canada), *Township Stories* (Edinburgh, London, national tour, Australian tour), *Things Fall Apart* (London, Washington DC, Lagos) and Hugh Masakela's *Songs of Migration* (London, Washington DC, South Africa).

Lighthouse 4O
CELEBRATING 40 YEARS IN POOLE

Lighthouse, Poole's Centre For The Arts is the UK's largest regional arts centre and Dorset's cultural centre of excellence for live performance, film and visual art. It is unique in that it is the only multi-space venue with four auditoria in the south west, housing a symphonic concert hall, mid-scale theatre, small-scale studio theatre, independent cinema, art galleries, and function room spaces. It is also home to the Bournemouth Symphony Orchestra. Lighthouse works in partnership with many organisations to present a richly diverse and bold programme of live performance, as well as nurturing and developing new work and artists. Its Sherling Studio is the only dedicated space in Dorset for supporting emerging talent across drama and many other genres. The venue's 80-20 vision allows it to act as a receiving venue of national importance whilst producing and co-producing a number of productions each year.

THE MARLOWE

The Marlowe, Canterbury, is one of the country's most successful regional theatres, bringing the work of prestigious companies such as The National Theatre, Royal Shakespeare Company, Matthew Bourne and Glyndebourne Opera to audiences in Kent. The Marlowe are committed to nurturing and inspiring creative talent with new writing at the heart of what they do. Roar, The Marlowe's new writing development programme, works to support writers and artists by providing the opportunity to develop bold and exciting new work through mentoring, workshops, funded research and development and work-in-progress sharings. Since reopening in 2011, The Marlowe has been committed to championing new writing and to date have been involved in the realisation of a number of productions that have gone on to be performed in London and around the country.

The Marlowe Roar Programme has been made possible with the support of The Marlowe Theatre Development Trust.

Supported using public funding by
ARTS COUNCIL ENGLAND

HANNAH AND HANNA
IN DREAMLAND

Cast

HANNAH

HANNA

All other characters played by Hannah and Hanna

HANNAH
aged 16, lives in Margate with her Nan,
who she looks after. Left school.

JOE
aged 22, her brother, a new policeman,
lives on the floor above.

NAN
aged 73, she has brought up Hannah and Joe
for the last seven years.

'BULLFROG'
aged 18, Hannah's bloke, unemployed.

HANNA (XHEVAHIRA)
aged 16, an ethnic Albanian asylum-seeker,
arrived from Kosovo.

ALBIN
aged 19, her brother, an engineering student
from Kosovo.

FLORA
aged 38, her mother, a recent widow,
a doctor in Kosovo.

Part 1

Part 1 takes place in Margate and Kosovo,
summer 1999 to spring 2000.

1999/2000

Summer 1999
NATO brings destruction of Kosovo to a halt
and Serbian leaders to justice.

Autumn 1999
1000 Kosovan refugees transported to Margate –
they are put up in unoccupied holiday accommadation.

Dover Express leader column
'We are left with the backdraft of a nation's human
sewage and no cash to wash it down the drain.'

Spring 2000
National Front march in Margate protesting
against immigration.

Summer 2000
Margate rated the cheapest places to buy a house
in the South East. .

PROLOGUE/Autumn 2018

Hannah and Hanna enter, each in a coat.
They are both in their mid-thirties.

Hannah and Hanna

We met in 1999.
We were both sixteen years old.

Hannah and Hanna remove their coats.

1

Hannah is English, brassily made up, with her hair up. Hanna,
Kosovan, is plainly dressed and wears no make-up. Each has
photographs that they show the audience in turn during the following.

Hannah

That's Margate from my window.

Hanna

That's Pristina, from the window of my old house.
Pristina is the capital city of Kosovo.

Hannah

That's me on the beach.
You can't see me because it's packed.

Hanna

That's me in a truck on its way from Kosovo to Dover.
You can't see me because I am hiding in the truck.

Hannah

That's the block of flats I live in with my Nan.

Hanna

That's the window of the room which I share with my
mother and my brother in the Hotel Bellevue in Margate.

Hannah

That's my brother Joe.
He's twenty-two and already a policeman.
Ugly, ain't he?

Hanna

This is my mother.
She sits all day looking at the sea from our window.

Hannah

And that's my bloke; everyone calls him Bullfrog –
Well, Bull to his face.

Hanna

And this is my brother Albin.
He walks around all day with the other young Kosovan guys.
They have nothing to do.
Handsome, isn't he?

Hannah

My name is Hannah.
I'm sixteen.
I've lived in Margate all my life.
Margate – what a town!
I hate it!

Hanna

My name is Hanna.
I'm sixteen.
I've lived in Margate for three days.
Margate – what a town!
I love it!

Hannah

Summer of ninety-nine.

July was crap.

August is scorching hot.

Hanna

This is my new home.

I fear nothing.

Hannah

The beaches are full of bodies.

So are the hotels, four or five to a room.

Hanna

Only thing I fear is leaving Margate.

Going home.

Hannah

But it's not like the old days.

The people on the beaches ain't the same as the people in the hotels.

Hanna

Three months of hiding in the mountains.

Three days in a lorry to England.

It is so nice to sleep in a bed.

Hannah

Bullfrog says, 'It's a bloody invasion,

Kosovo arrived here in the night!'

That pretty much sums up the feeling locally.

Hanna

My family lost everything.

Except our freedom.

When we arrived in Dover I kissed the ground.

Free.

At last.

Hannah

Sets up karaoke machine during the following:

Picture this:
I'm down on the sea-front
With Bull and all his mates,
Doing what I do best
On a hot summer night.

2

Hannah is singing 'I SHOULD BE SO LUCKY'/KYLIE MINOGUE on her karaoke machine with 'HANNAH' written upon it in large capitals. Hannah ad-libs so the audience sees she is performing for an onstage 'audience' with whom she interacts either to insult (in reaction to their taunts) or flirt or show off.

Hanna moves towards Hannah, watching her performance. Hannah spots Hanna and continues to sing. Then she stops singing, with the tape still playing and herself still moving to the song.

The song is interspersed with the following dialogue:

Hannah
Are you another one of them?

Hanna is blank.

Thought you were somehow, something in the air

She sniffs.

What can it be?
It's a sort of foreign smell – maybe it ain't you.
It must be the scum that comes in with the tide at night.

She sings again, then breaks off.

You still standing there?

Where you from then?
Outer Mongolia?

Hanna is blank.

Timbucbloodytoo?

Hanna is blank

Hannah switches off tape.

Don't tell me
I spy with my little eye someone beginning with 'K'.

Hannah gets a laugh from her 'audience' for this.

Hanna still blank

K-K-K-Kosovo…?

Hanna looks down as if ashamed.

Ain't you got a tongue in your head?

Hannah takes in her friends laughing with her.

Hanna silent.

Well, come on then Kosovan Spice, say something – or
die…

Hanna silent.

*Hannah walks over to her and puts the microphone to Hanna's
mouth.*

OK, what's your name?

Hanna
My name is Hanna.

Hannah
What!?

Oh very funny!

To Bull and her mates.

That ain't her real name
They're all bloody liars
Don't you know that much?
Oh you can all sod off!

It's gone wrong – she exits, angry.

Hanna *(to audience)*
My real name is Xhevahira ('Jerve-a-heera')
But no one can pronounce it here.
My middle name is Hanna,
So here in Margate my mother named me again.
Hanna – because of all our sorrow,
And because it would help me to make friends in England.
I didn't mean to take her name.

3

Hannah
Cliftonville is a mile up from Margate.
It's all posh hotels and lawns
Looking over the sea.
There's a bowling green there
where Bull and I always go
when it's hot and it's dark.
But I just wasn't in the mood…

I was bloody furious, wouldn't you be?
It's MY name and I ain't sharing it with an asylum-seeker!

Suddenly Bull's off on one.

(as Bull)
'Bloody Kosovans
Come over to Dover.
Nick yer house, your car, your girlfriend,
Fill their trolleys to the brim
And get a hundred pound a week –
For what?
To have a lovely seaside holiday – for a year!
We should be so lucky.
That Kosovitch!
I'd tell her straight –
Go back home
'n' give her a slap next time…'

(as Hannah)
That's my boy
I'm the only Hannah round here aren't I?

She reacts as if Bull moves towards her.

Come here, Bull.
Where would I be without you?

As Hannah exits, she squeals in pleasure.

4

Hanna

I go home and I am upset because the English don't like me.
Mother is crying in our room.
The sun is shining and she's crying.
My brother won't stay in our room.
He does not like her crying.
He goes out on the street all the day.
He walks in a gang to be safe

Kosovan gang – English gang – very bad.
I don't like this English girl.
But I like how she sings.

Pause.

I sing too
I know all the songs as well as her.
Everyone in Pristina knows English music.
I like Britney Spears, All Saints, Westlife, Celine Dion, Steps.

She sings 'TRAGEDY'/STEPS for a full minute, voice and gesture perfect, no accompaniment.

Some people here are stupid.
They don't like us but they don't know us.
But Joe the policeman who protects our hotel,
He is smiling and he makes jokes.
He makes us feel safe.

I am going to make the shopping
In Aldi's.

5

Hanna sets up the counter at Aldi supermarket.

Hannah *(in overalls)*
Aldi's – it's where I work on a Saturday and Thursday night.
Everyone goes there.
It's the cheapest shop in Margate.
Last Thursday I'm standing behind the counter,
There's a massive queue
It's one of our busiest nights
And guess who holding everyone up?

(to Hanna)
Got an Aldi's card?

Hanna
No.

Hannah
Cashback?

Hanna
No.

She holds out a voucher.

Hannah peers at Hanna's full basket.

You can only spend ten pounds with one of these you know.
Can't buy the whole shop.

Hanna
I have vouchers for myself, my brother and my mother.
That's thirty pounds.

Hannah
Your mother and your brother here are they?

Hanna
No they are at home.

Hannah
Where's that then?

Hanna
Here, in Margate.
I live here you know.

Hannah
I thought your home was in Kosovo.
Margate's my home not yours.

You people just don't seem to realize that
However many times you're told it,
Do you?

Hanna

I came here to buy food, not listen again to you.
Please stop your talking.

Hannah

One voucher buys ten pound of shopping,
No change.
One person one voucher for one week.
You'll have to put it back
Or bring the rest of the family in.
Call them on your mobile

Hanna

I have not got a mobile.

Hannah

You've all got mobiles.

Hanna

I have no phone, I have no pounds.
I take the bread the butter the jam the apples the oranges the
coffee the sugar the oil the ham the shampoo seven pounds
and five pence the banana the washing powder the asprin
the Coca-Cola – that's nine pounds and fifty-seven pence...

Hannah

No change.

Hanna

The baked beans.

Hannah

Nine pounds and eighty pence, get some matches and
start a fire.

Hanna

You have the money,
why don't you set fire to yourself!

Hannah and Hanna to audience

Hanna

She has no right to talk to me like that.

Hannah

You'd think she owned the bloody place the way she
carries on.

Hanna

A lady in the queue said at least I stood up for myself.

Hannah

Next time I won't give her the chance.

6

*Hannah sings 'HIT ME BABY ONE MORE TIME'/BRITNEY
SPEARS with the karaoke player to the same crowd that she did Kylie
for. Hanna joins in for a sustained period, singing really well, until
Hannah can stand it no longer. The karoake machine continues playing:*

Hannah

Shut up!
I don't want to sing with you, talk to you
Or live in the same bloody town as you!
I don't want to breathe the same air as you people
So fuck off and stop stalking me round,
You freaky foreign person.
I don't want to see you again –
Alright?

Hanna stares at her.

Don't stand there pretending you're a human.
You're Kosovan, that's a foreign word, means scum.

Hanna turns and leaves.

Hannah turns to her audience.

What are you all staring at?
No surrender.
Like you said, ay, Bull?

Hannah exits.

7

Hanna

I am in England and I'm crying.
I tell my mother what happened;
She holds me in her arms.
Then she makes me sit down and she talks to me.
She sits upright in her chair, like this...

Hanna becomes her mother.

It's very hot so she's fanning herself.
The manager still hasn't fixed the window.
She talks to me a bit like a doctor talking to a patient.
That's what she is in Pristina, a doctor.
This is what she says to me in our language – in Albanian:

(as her mother)
"As you know, your father loved the English language,
But most of all he loved the English people.
English was his life and his work;
He taught the language very well
And after the Serbs sacked him
He only had one student left –

You, his darling girl.
But there is one thing you must not forget.
Your father could talk all day about England –
Westminster, Brighton Pier, FA Cup, Tony Blair –
But he never came to England.
He never left Kosovo!
Unlike you, he never saw the sea,
Only mountains…
You know what I'm saying, don't you?
Kosovo was invaded and crushed for ten years.
He would say, 'The English never let this happen to England!'
Your father imagined the English to be so good,
So honourable, so courageous, so decent.
Well, of course
There never was a people like that anywhere.
I don't like the English who call us names
And if your father was alive and in Margate,
Neither would he."

It's no use listening to my mother.
She thinks in Kosovan.
What am I supposed to do?
Stay in all day?

Hanna exits.

8

Hannah
I go home.
I'm churned up.
Just who does she think she is?
I'd never been as hard as that before on anyone.
I had this sickly feeling in my gut…

Hannah acts out the following.

I stop off at the library and get Nan's books
Nan's who I live with because me mum ain't around.
I pick up the washing from the laundrette,
Almost forget her paper.
Climb eleven floors with the washing and the books,
Cos the lift's still ain't fixed.

'Hallo, Nan.'

Pause.

'Course it's me,
who else is it gonna be?'

Nan's sitting in her chair,
Curtains drawn as usual
The room smells of – I dunno –
But it smells.
I give her her paper.

'Nan you've got to start going out again
It's beautiful outside
You look like a ghost.'

Tell you the truth
I can't stand being in the place with her.
But Joe's busy and if I don't do the necessaries
She'd fade away in her chair.
All you'd see is the *Margate Gazette.*
Muggers, drivers, robbers, prampushers 'n' dogwalkers
She's afraid of them all

(as Nan)
"Hannah!
They've put my letter in the paper.

The one about the pensioners.
The *Margate Gazette* is a good paper, you know.
They've put my letter near the top
By a picture of the Home Secretary.
'Is he listening to Margate?' it says"

'Yeh, lovely Nan,
But don't you think it's more important that you go out?'

She's about to lecture me about why she lives indoors all
the time
But instead
My brother Joe makes a visit,
Looking very smart in his uniform.
As usual, he says,

(as Joe)
'Don't go up to Cliftonville tonight, Hannah, I'm telling you.
There'll be trouble and I don't want you involved –
Right?'

'Right you are, Joe, never trust me, do you?'

(to audience)
Course I'll be there.
It's Saturday night.
Keep me head low from Joe –
He can smell smoke on me breath at fifty paces.
But in this town trouble's a magnet.
What else is there to look for in Margate?
It's a year-round rumble for having to live in the place –
And now we can hit Kosovans
'Stead of each other.
I wanna go there
So I'll end up there,
Joe or no Joe
Magnetic, see?

9

'RIGHT HERE RIGHT NOW'/FATBOY SLIM.

Choreographed dance sequence representing a street fight.

Hanna
Saturday night in Cliftonville.

Hannah
Same street.

Hanna
Same wall.

Hannah
Same aggro bubbling under.
Bull's there – finished work at six – had four pints by eight.
It's a hot night.
He's in shorts – shades
And a shirt with KOSOVILLE on it in letters of dripping blood.

Hanna
Albin and his friends are bored of being told to go home.
They decide to walk across the road,
Play a football game.

Hannah
Nine-a-side,
Shirts for goal posts,
Stripped to the waist – 'n' off they go –
Kosovan asylum-seeker team A vs Kosovan asylum-seeker team B.

Hanna
The Kosovans play football very good.
All the girls see that, so the boys do too, I know.

Hannah

Nothing happens, we're quite happy to watch the game.
Then whose idea is it to nick the bloody ball?

Hanna

Her stupid ugly boyfriend runs onto the grass,
Puts the ball under his arm and runs towards the cliff.

Hannah

Off goes Bull followed by eighteen Kosovan lads,
Each one barechested and with a knife in his pocket,
Screaming blue murder, in Albanian,
Chased by another thirty Margate kids;
Then two coppers, screaming into their radios for help...

Hanna

Ugly boy reaches the clifftop,
Kicks the ball up into the air,
Down into the sea below.

Hannah

Hang on,
The ball goes up into the air but not down into the sea.
It hovers, seems to stop and have a think, changes its mind –
And falls onto the tarmac into the middle of fifty panting
youths.

Hanna

Albin jumps up and catches it
And off he goes running like the wind,
Back over the grass,
Across the road
Down Ethelred Crescent –
Fifty of us chasing the ball in Albin's hands –
Why?

I don't *know* why
But I can't stop running…

Hannah

Bull's running across the tops of cars –
His favourite trick.
The dog-walkers and pram-pushers dive for cover
And a lady with a stick goes flying across the pavement.
Someone screams and there's a crash of glass.
On we go,
Into the road;
Cars screech out the way –

Hannah and Hanna

CRASH!

Hanna

The car hits the lamp post and stops,
The post like this…
I don't stop
I don't care, I just run and run,
Faster now,
Down the hill;
There's more than fifty of us now.

Hannah

A bus swerves;
it nearly, oh-so-nearly, goes flat upon its side.
You should have heard the screams inside –
Loud enough to wake the dead of Margate!

Hanna

We turn a corner and I see the beach, the bay, the lights.
Many, many people too.
For one second I see Albin

Still in front, his face a knife;
Then on he goes, he's gone.

Hannah

In the dying light I see 'bout eighty – more –
For one second I thought –
If the Kosovans need Margate –
Margate needs the Kosovans!
When last did we have such a time as *this?*

Hanna

Faster and faster
Down the hill to the beach, I can't stop running –
My legs are moving faster;
I can't stop my legs!
Onto the sand –

Hannah

We hit the beach.
The Kosovan with the ball stops.

Hanna

Albin kicks it in the air.

Hannah

It lands in the sea and bobs about on the tide.

Hanna

The stupidest fight you've ever seen begins.

Hannah and Hanna

All in slow motion…

Hannah

The breath has gone from everybody.
The sand soaks up the action.

They flop.

Hanna
Hands on knees.
Ugly boy is moving through the gasping bodies
He's moving towards Albin.
Albin doesn't see him.

Hannah
I look up to see Bull land a heavy punch
To the head of the Kosovan who carried the ball.

Hanna
He drops like a stone.

Hannah
Everyone around Bull's cheering
Bull's goin' mad.

Hanna
He's kicking Albin in the head.
Albin!

Hannah
Bull! What'd'ya think you're doing?!

Hanna *(screams)*
Albin!

Hannah *(screams)*
Bull!

They mime pulling Bull off Albin.

Hannah and Hanna
Get off! Get off! Get off!

Hannah turns and sees her brother.

Hanna sees her beloved policeman.

Hanna

Look it's the policeman from our hotel...
Look! Look!

Hannah

Joe! Joe!
Pull him off before he kills him!

They mime pulling Bull off Albin, their actions stylized and identical.

Joe had him in an arm-lock and out of view in seconds flat.
I saw him and a woman copper take him off

Hanna

Albin was still and bleeding from his nose and head.

Hanna turns to address Hannah.

Please... Hannah...

Hannah turns reluctantly to Hanna.

Please help me lift him up.
I have to take him home.

Hannah

You'll never get him back up to Cliftonville.
We've just run a mile and a half downhill.
Just wait for an ambulance.

Hanna

If they think he's making all this trouble
They put him in prison till he goes back to Kosovo.
Please please help.
It's your boyfriend who beat him.

Hannah *(to audience)*
There was fighting and screaming all around us.

21

Her brother started groaning.
I said
'OK
My flat's crap but it's near the beach
Come with me.'

Hanna
I will.
Thank you Hannah.

Hannah *(to audience)*
Sometimes you just gotta grit your teeth, don't you?

10

'BY THE RIVER'/GROOVE ARMADA.

Hannah and Hanna carry Albin across the road to the tower block.

Hannah presses the bell of the intercom.

Hannah
Hi Nan it's me.
No, I've got my key.
I'm just bringing two visitors up, ok?
No, you don't know them.
Look, one of them's hurt, ok?
Is the lift – ?
Good!

(to audience)
We put him in the lift, I was shaking.
We get to my door.
Nan's standing there.
She screams her head off.
I ain't ever heard her scream before.

Goes to her room
And slams the door.

Hanna
We made Albin comfortable.
Then we saw each other.
We were both covered in blood.

(to Hannah)
Keep him awake.
I won't be long.

Hannah
Where are you going?

Hanna
To get my mother.
She knows what to do.

Hanna exits

Hannah
You can't leave me here...

(to audience.)
The front door slams.
She's gone.
Nan's door opens.
Her head peeps round
'Have they gone?' she says.
Out she comes,
Slap into Albin
Bleeding over her favourite chair...
I almost died.
She don't move or say nothing.
Then

'We better clean the poor sod up, hadn't we?
His mother can't see him like this.'
And she takes over, fussing over Albin – he was Albin now –
Like he was her own…
She dabbed and wiped.
Albin groaned in pain.
Then the buzzer went.

Hanna
My mother walks in.

Hannah
She's not what I expected.
No headscarf no anorak,
She smells of nice perfume.
She's quite a lady.
She checks over Albin,
Very professional,
Then gives him a big cuddle.
She smiles at Nan, who almost curtseys.
Then Hanna's mother trys to thank my Nan…

Hanna (as Mother to Nan)
'You..very..good..English..dame'

Hannah
Before now,
Nan thought Kosovans were a bunch of hooligans.

(as Nan to Mother)
'Your English ain't up to much is it, love?'

(to audience)
She's very impressed.
Offers her a cup of tea.

Hanna *(as Mother)*

'Thank you madam.'

Hannah

Then Joe turns up and is about to start on me.

Nan butts in, quite posh,

'Don't start now Joe

We've got some visitors from abroad.'

Hanna

We see the figure of a policeman at the door.

The asylum-seekers turn to stone.

We feel guilty.

It's automatic.

Hannah's grandmother introduces him as Joe, her grandson.

It's him,

The policeman from our hotel,

The policeman on the beach,

The angel policeman.

Albin nods to him very polite.

Mother shakes his hand.

I stand staring like I do.

Hannah

I've got that sickly feeling in my gut again.

I feel dizzy.

Hanna

I'm glad to be here.

Everyone safe.

Albin is on his feet,

Mother smiling,

And I've found Hannah

Without even looking for her.

She's standing by the doorway now.

I can't see her face.

Hannah

I watch them sitting, three Kosovans,

An angry pensioner and a policeman –

Why can't I let go and enjoy the party too?

Hanna

I translate for Albin and for my mother.

Her name is Flora which makes them laugh

Because in England it means margerine.

Hannah's grandmother asked us if we will come back next
Friday

And of course my mother says we will.

This is the first time mother has left the hotel

Since we arrived,

The first time she has used

The English that she knows.

Albin doesn't speak

But I know he understands.

He is quiet with the policeman

It was Albin who had the ball…

After some time we say goodbye and thank you

Many times.

Hannah comes out of the shadow…

(to Hannah)

Do you mind if I come and see you again?

Hannah

Yeh

When you come

We could do a song or something in my room, ok?

Hanna

Thank you, Hannah.

Hannah *(to audience)*

Go on, hate me, I do, I just wanted to do something,
Something nice like everyone else seemed to be doing.
And it made my stomach feel better.
So it was the right thing
For me to do
At the time,
Right?

11

'TORN'/NATALIE IMBRUGLIA.

Hannah and Hanna sing to the CD; at first Hannah is cool towards Hanna. Hanna refuses to be patronized. They take time to thaw and though the singing is good, it takes until the end of the song for the girls to be at ease with each other and to sing together with full energy.

After singing together for two verses and a chorus:

Hanna
What do you want to be when you grow up?

Hannah
I wanna be rich.
What about you?

Hanna
I want to be a pharmacist.

Hannah
Oh

Music fades.

Hannah *(to audience)*
All this leaves out Bullfrog.
I couldn't tell him about Hanna and me.

He'd turn into a one-man mental institution.
I liked him.
Till that night on the beach
When he tasted blood.
Once Hanna walked past me and Bull on the front
And I had to do it.
I had to pretend I was the same as I was before

Shouting directly at Hanna.

KOSOVO. SCUM. GO BACK HOME!

Pause.

I'm so sorry.
Bull was there.
I had to do it.
I'm really sorry, Hanna.

Hanna
It's OK.
In my country it happens all the time.

Hannah
Things have changed.
Me and Hanna are like Nan now.

Hanna
Like Nan *was.*

Hannah
Oh yeah.
Nan goes out now.
All by herself.

Hanna
Mother and Albin and Joe all meet for tea on Fridays.

Hannah

My Nan's set up the Kosovan branch of the Women's Institute!

If Bull finds out,

I'll be the one needing asylum.

Hanna

She worries too much.

I love being in her flat.

Eleven floors up looking over the sea.

We are singing every day.

No one can see us.

No one can hear us.

Movement to indicate passage of time and intense practice.

Hannah

It was getting boring, staying in.

So we went out,

Sang on the front.

Bull was there.

But I weren't bothered.

We just sung

Our favourite song.

Hannah urges the anxious Hanna on to the platform.

Hannah and Hanna sing and dance a perfected version of 'PERFECT'/FAIRGROUND ATTRACTION.

This is a real performance piece the girls have worked on for weeks.

Music of original track begins.

Hannah and Hanna dance prepared routine.

As the song performance ends, both put on caps and they play Bullfrog in unison.

Hannah and Hanna *(as Bullfrog)*

Gotcha!

Asylum lover.

Kosovo lesbo.

Margate bloody traitor.

English scum.

You come out on the front again,

You're dead.

Hear that?

Dead.

Hannah,

Bloody Hannah:

Dead

Right?

Dead.

Hannah and Hanna exit separately.

12

Four months later: music and movement to convey the passage of time.

Hannah

One night, just before Christmas,

Bull and his mates – his 'bully-boys' as he likes to call 'em –

They ambushed us as we came out the main door of the flats.

But it was me they wanted to hurt, not Hanna.

Piano version of 'GOOD KING WENCESLAS'.

Choreographed sequence in which Hannah is spat at, kicked and trodden by Hanna as Bull.

Hanna *(as herself)*

I sit in the library because it is warm and I read English books.

We don't meet anymore,

Not even in secret.
Hannah is hurt.
She is afraid of Bull now.
I know very well how she is feeling
But I miss her.
I haven't seen her for days.

Hannah

I've stopped going out just for the time being.
It's pretty horrible out there anyway.
Joe keeps an eye on our door, which is nice.
When the lift broke again I asked Joe not to get it fixed.
I feel safer up here that way.
Anyway, whenever I bin out lately,
I was getting, 'English scum – asylum-lover',
All that crap in my ears.
And it weren't just me.
Joe got it too.
Once word got out about Nan's Friday tea parties,
He had the piss taken once too often.
Joe ended up in a fight himself over it.
Nan didn't like both of us getting grief.
So she closed down the tea parties.
Now Nan moans at *me* for never going out.
But she looks after me,
Just like I looked after her.

When the rain beats on the windows all through the afternoon,
All I can see is grey shite and seagulls.

Hannah reads a letter from Hanna.

Hanna

Mother stays in all day now.
I cannot make her go out.

She cannot work here even though she is a children's doctor.
Mother and Albin get more and more sad together.
When the weather is very bad
I take my walkman to the beach.
With the rain in my face,
I forget everyone and everything.
I try and see you at your window
But it's too far away.
Maybe you can see me.
When I get in from the storm outside,
The room feels warmer.
Mother and Albin are sleeping.
They sleep hours every day,
Dreaming of leaving,
Dreaming of home.

Hanna reads a letter from Hannah.

Hannah
Bull is sending nasty stuff in the mail,
Really evil stuff, some of it.
I don't know what's happened to his sense of humour.
He's obsessed.
And since things are quieter at your hotel,
Joe spends more time keeping an eye on my door
Than he does on yours.
Bull seems to think I'm the asylum-seeker now,
So it's me who gets the treatment.
Cos I don't hate you,
He hates me.
It's stupid and it's doing my bloody head in.
Every time I think I'll go out,
I wanna be sick.

Joe got into trouble for that scrap I told you about.
Nearly lost his job.
Coppers can't get into punch ups,
It's illegal.
He's going to do something about it, he says,
But he won't say what –
You'll see, he says, you'll see…
The longer I stay in,
The harder it is to go out.
I'll come and see you soon,
Promise.

Hannah reads a letter from Hanna.

13

Hanna

I have big news!
Joe is driving a lorry to Pristina.
He is taking medicines to hospitals,
And as my mother is a doctor,
She may be allowed to go with him!
And Albin!
And ME!
I don't want to go back to bloody Kosovo!
But nobody listens to me.

Hannah

Nan always said,
Joe's a good deed
And you're a bad deed.
Bloody Joe!

(to Hanna as Joe)
Joe!

Hanna *(as Joe)*
What?

Hannah
You didn't tell me!

Hanna *(as Joe)*
What?

Hannah *(waving letter)*
This!

Hanna *(as Joe)*
Sorry, I had to ask them first, didn't I?

Hannah
You can't leave me alone in Margate!

Hanna *(as Joe)*
People miss you, you know that?

Hannah
I don't miss them!

Hanna *(as Joe)*
You can't lock yourself up in here forever.
You gotta face the world again, Hannah.

Hanna gives letter to Hannah.

Hannah opens letter.

Hanna
We are leaving next week.
My mother is so happy she can't stop smiling.
I want to see you to say goodbye.

Hannah
Thing is, somehow, we're best friends...

Even though I never see Hanna,
I can't face not seeing her again.

Hanna

Can we meet by the clock tower at twelve tomorrow?

Hannah *(to audience)*

I know it's stupid but like my Nan
I've built up this fear of going out.
Of course, like her, I'll go out and I won't see what I fear.
I won't see Bull or his mates.
I'll just walk up to the clock tower and we'll jump about,
And then we'll go up to the hotel together,
And I'll wave them off to Kosovo.
Sad how I feel jealous of an asylum-seeker
For leaving Margate…
I used to think they were lucky to be here.

Hannah leaves the flat.

I go out.
It's a hot spring day like you get now.
I feel fabulous,
like Hanna said she felt when she got here last summer.
Nan has put some sandwiches in a bag for me
And made me promise I'll be home by four.
Don't worry I said,
I'll probably be home for lunch
And eat them on the sofa.
'You'll eat them alone,' she said 'I'm out today.'
(She's never in these days, my Nan)

I walk along the front.
I feel I'm flying.
Here I am,

Free again and newly-born.
A second later,
I hear the chant I hate and fear –
'KOSOVANS GO HOME
GO BACK HOME.'
'Cept this time it ain't just Bull,
But what sounds like a pubfull of monster blokes.
My stomach churns with fear.
I feel I'm being told to go back home.
Instantly, I want to run back to the flat.
I turn and there they are –
The National Front in triumph straggling along Sea Road.
They've brought kiddies too,
boy nazis and toy nazis,
All bellowing down the front at no one in particular.
Just a load of coppers and bored Margate people staring.
I'm standing there taking it in,
and I hear OUT, OUT, OUT chanted from behind me.
Yes, it's the other mob, the Anti-Nazi League,
Coming towards me!
They're arm-in-arm, all shapes and sizes –
And in the front line,
My Nan!
The Kosovans have turned my family inside out!
Joe going there today in a truck,
Me Nan fighting the National Front.
What have I been doing all winter?
I want to help Nan or save her or something.
But when I look at her
Her head held high and her looking so proud,
I want to hide away again.
I turn and run.

In panic I slip,
Arse over tit in the path of the National Front.
And I'm looking up at Bull,
Ugly bastard in a T-shirt
With a Union Jack turned into a bloody Swastika across
the front,
Yelling ENGLAND FOR THE ENGLISH.
A second later he'd see me.
This time, I get in first

Mimes kicking Bull in the balls

CRUNCH!
He went 'ENGLAND FOR THE – Arrghh…'
I heard it but I didn't see.
I was gone.

14

'BETTER OFF ALONE'/ALICE DJ continues through following.

Hanna
Jumping up and down by a lamp post, wanting to see and not be seen.
It's twelve o'clock and there is a war starting around me.
This is the place we said we'd meet –
Hannah hurry please hurry Hannah!

She mimes Hannah zooming past – shouts after her.

HANNAH!

'BETTER OFF ALONE'/ALICE DJ surges.

Hannah and Hanna create a chase in profile.

They both get to the lorry.

Hannah jumps onto lorry and hides inside it – is not seen by Hanna.

Hanna

I've lost her.

She's not at the hotel.

She's not by the lorry.

Joe is shouting at me that we're leaving NOW!

Mother and Albin are waving at me.

The National Front are coming up the hill,

I don't want to leave.

I don't want to leave.

Hanna sits down in the front of the lorry.

Hannah is hidden in the back.

The lorry departs with both aboard.

We've left.

We're going down the hill

In a lorry with KOSOVO AID written along its side.

Spit hits the window by my head.

I look at the beach and the sea for a last second.

I'm looking everywhere for Hannah.

We drive past the back of the sign that says

WELCOME TO MARGATE.

She's gone.

I can't see her…

I've lost her.

Where was she running?

Why was she running from me?

Hannah

I can't see a thing in here.

It's totally black.

I want to scream my bloody head off

But then I'd give myself away.

No one's going to find me here.
No one.

Hanna

Dover.
I remember Dover.
Three days and three nights in a lorry to get here.
We were hidden in the back all that time.
There were twelve of us and a baby.
The mother put her hand hard over his mouth,
Every time we stopped.
There was a hole in the top for light.
A hole in the floor for toilet.
We paid three thousand pounds to come to Dover.
Everything that my father left to us.
When the door opened on the third night
We put up our hands.
We thought we would be shot.
The man said 'Get out now' and we did.
Then he drove away.
I did not know what country we were standing in,
Till I saw the sign for Dover.

Hannah

I've been sleeping for hours.
I don't know what time it is.
I finished my sandwiches ages ago.
I've kept the chocolate for emergency.
But I'm starving.
There's a plastic bin to pee in
But no lid.
Nan will be home by now.
She'll think I'm a dirty stop-out.

Hanna

Calais, Dunkirk, Zeebrugge, Ghent,
Brussells, Aachen, Cologne.
Albin is driving now.
Mother wants me to sing but I can't.
I left my voice in Margate.
Everything I want to forget,
I remember like yesterday.
Nuremberg, Passau, Graz, Leibnitz...

Hannah

I'm turning into a cockroach in here
A blind dirty thing that lives in the dark.
I'm not coming out.
I'm not coming out.
They can lock me up or beat me up,
I'm going all the way.

Hanna

We stop, we start again, on and on and on.
We are always crossing borders.
I go to sleep in Hungary,
wake in Romania.
The lorry is moving but I am not moving.
I am sleeping in the Hotel Bellevue,
Dreaming we are driving,
Driving...
Dreaming...

'WAKE UP HANNA WAKE UP!'

My mother is shaking me.

Hanna wakes up, doesn't know what's happening, where she is.

'LOOK! KOSOVO!'

I've been stuck so long in my seat,
I don't know that we are moving.
I open the door to step out of the lorry,
My mother grabs onto my coat.
I am falling out of my coat.
Joe is shouting and stopping the lorry.
I fall out of my coat into the road –
I don't want to be in Kosovo!
LET ME OUT LET ME OUT

She is crying and sobbing and on her knees.

Hannah

I was thrown out of my corner into the darkness.
My toilet bucket spilt over.
I was wet through.
I can't stand it anymore!
LET ME OUT LET ME OUT

Hannah and Hanna

Both are on their knees.
LET ME OUT!
LET ME OUT!

Hannah

The big doors open and there's Joe!
'Hannah! What the hell are you doing here?'
'Oh Joe – I'm seeking asylum from Margate!'

Hannah and Hanna

And there was Hanna/h

Hannah and Hanna reunite ecstatically.

*Crossfade KOSOVAN FOLK SONG over their voices till they
are silent.*

Hannah

I washed in a river.
I stuffed my face with food.
Hanna lent me a clean top.

Hanna

I was ready to jump,
But Hannah is here.
I am in Kosovo,
But Hannah is here.
I cannot believe it.
I cannot believe it.

They fall asleep across one another.

Kosovan music continues to play.

15

Hannah

We woke up.
I think we woke up anyway.
Everything seemed slower and brighter.
I don't know how we were standing
By the side of the road
And no longer in the lorry...
That's where we were.
It was getting dark.
Hanna and me were staring at a coach.

Hanna

That's the coach.

Hannah

A dead coach, you could say.
It was all brown and black

Brown with rust and black from fire,
Parked by itself on this empty road,
Mountains all around.

Hanna

We left for Macedonia in that coach.
It was our escape from Kosovo.
The beginning of our journey to Margate.
We were stopped by the Serbs.
They were selecting young people.
Albin and I were both chosen.
My mother was still in that coach
They would not let her off.
The men were taken off first,
The women were taken to a garage
Twenty minutes down the road,
A big empty building.
The soldiers all had knives and guns,
All were wearing masks.
My clothes were torn off me.

She pauses.

At some point the screaming around me stopped.
I think the soldiers got some sort of order,
I do not know why they set us free.
We were taken out of the garage back to the roadside.
We smelt the coach burning before we saw it.
We met up again with the men.
Albin was there and though he was beaten,
He was standing.
He was alive.
I was ashamed for him to see me like this.
But he saw I was alive too.

Not all of the men were there.
The coach was still in flames.
The Serbs made us walk – to Macedonia…
I did not know if my mother was dead in the coach.
When I got to the camp in Macedonia I was very bad.
My mother was waiting for us.
She was alive.
She looked after us.
She helped me not to be ashamed.
I cried for weeks and my mother said,
'Don't stop – cry more' and hugged me.
When Albin told me about a lorry going to England,
He said it was the first time that I smiled again.
We could go to England.

(to Hannah)
Sorry to make you sad.

Hannah says nothing.

Say something.

Hannah says nothing.

'Ain't you got a tongue in your head?'

Hannah
I'd want to kill the people who did that to me.

Hanna
That's what Albin wants to do.
That's why he's come back.
But I do not want that.

Hannah
I feel useless.

Hanna

You're not.
You're here.

Hannah

I called you scum.

Hanna

I fought back…

Hannah

I feel sick.
I wish I was in Margate.

Hanna

So do I.
So much.

Hannah

Come back.
I'm not frightened anymore,
And neither should you be.
They can call us what names they bloody like.
I know what I'll say.

Hanna

Right…

Hannah

I know!
We'll sing…
Sing together!
Become a group,
Get on *Top of the Pops* or something –
Right?

Hanna

Right.

I can't come.

Hannah

Nan'll put you up...

Hanna

I'm not allowed back.

Hannah

Sez who?

Hanna

Once you leave you can't go back.

Only if I've got loads of money.

Or I marry an English guy...

Hannah

Marry Joe...

They laugh.

Hannah

Look –

If you can't come to Margate

I'll stay here with you for a while.

Nan can manage by herself for a bit.

Wha'd'ya say?

Hanna

Did you bring your passport?

Hannah

Passport?

No.

I ain't got one.

I ain't never bin abroad before.

Hanna drops her head.

I'm sorry about what you told me.
I'm sorry it happened to you.
I'm sorry.

Hanna

Why haven't you got a passport?
Then you could stay for a bit.
I wish I had a British passport.
I could live in Margate,
I wouldn't have to be here in Kosovo
And live with people who want to kill each other.

You don't see Margate like me.
It is a beautiful town.
One day other people will go there,
And they will see it too.

Hannah turns and faces Hanna.

Hannah

Is this it?

Hanna

Yes.
This is it.

*Hannah and Hanna sing 'TORN'/NATALIE AMBRUGLIA
unaccompanied. They hold hands.*

They exit separately.

END OF PART 1

Part 2

Part 2 takes place in Pristina, Margate and Calais.

In 2008 Kosovo became an independent European state.

SUMMER 2015

March 2015
UKIP conference at Winter Gardens.

June 2015
Dreamland re-opens.

July 2015
Calais Jungle reaches 9000 migrants reflecting
greatest refugee exodus to Western Europe
since World War 2.

October 2015
The Times lists Margate as one of the thirty most
fashionable places to live in the UK.

SECOND PROLOGUE/Autumn 2018

Hannah and Hanna enter each in a coat.

Hannah and Hanna
We met again in 2015
We were both thirty-two.

Hannah and Hanna remove their coats.

16

Hannah and Hanna are now fifteen years older.

Hannah is an estate agent, dressed stylishly in suit and heels.

Hanna is more casual, in jeans but with bright beret.

Hannah
This is Margate from my window.
Margate from the window of my car.
My new Phelps and Phelps branded
Mini Cooper two-door hardtop.
I see two towns – both called Margate.
One is the dump I should have left long ago.
The other is the one I sell to people…
Do I see a grey shitty house in a street with an abandoned
sofa on the pavement
Overflowing dustbins and loose cables flapping in the wind,
Dog shit and slime and broken bottles on the steps?
Is that what I see?
Or do I see a Victorian six-bedroomed townhouse
with commanding views over the North Sea?

A magnificent early nineteenth-century dwelling in the centre of Margate?

I see the Margate it pays to see.

I thought I'd never make any money in this dump.

But now I sell Margate

Brick by golden brick.

Hanna

This is Pristina from my window –

The window of the City Hospital Emergency Unit.

I work here.

It's where my mother was a doctor

Before she died.

I should have been a doctor like my mother,

Or at least a pharmacist.

But I didn't have the money for studying.

So I'm a driver.

I drive ambulances.

I'm the first woman ambulance driver in Kosovo.

Hannah

Couple of months ago, I sang 'My Heart Will Go On'
at a Celine Dion tribute night at The Walpole.

I still sing now and then.

This blazer walks in while I'm singing and when I've finished
He keeps on clapping,

Buys me a large one and suggests I might like to sing at his
conference.

He says he's just the song for me,

Written for the occasion and it's in a calypso style –

I say, 'No problem for me, I'd love to do it!'

He roars, 'And we'll pay you, you know!'

I say, 'All the better! Who's the conference for?'

'UKIP', he says

'I've heard of them – what is UKIP exactly?'

We introduce ourselves.

Nigel explains that he's the leader of the party.

This was getting really interesting.

In a few words, he explained what they stood for.

I say, 'Well it makes a lot of sense to me – but I don't think my Nan would approve!'

He just laughed.

Insisted I had another large one!

He really seemed to like me.

During the above, Hannah sets up her microphone and stand to practice her gig for the UKIP conference.

Brief recorded sounds from the 2015 UKIP conference.

Out of the blue,

Hanna turns up again on Facebook.

Sends me a friend request.

For some reason I accept.

I don't know why.

She's done this before

And, to tell the truth,

I've ignored her.

I put her out of my mind when I got back home fifteen years ago.

I had so much shit to take from Bull and his mates!

I put my past behind me

That was that.

Now she's messaged to say she'll be in Margate for a few days…

I asked her to come along to the The Winter Gardens…

She might catch me doing my number!

Hannah appears at the UKIP conference.

She performs two verses and the chorus of 'UKIP Calypso' by Mike Reid.

Hannah takes a bow to big applause for her performance.

17

Hanna
Just like the first time I saw her!
Hannah singing.
They love her…

Hannah
And there is Hanna,
Standing on her own in the middle of the crowd
Waving at me.

They meet again.

Hanna
Hannah! You look so chic, so confident…

Hannah
And you haven't changed at all!

Hanna
But you are so sophisticated!

Hannah
I get a lot of buyers come here from London – don't wanna look too shabby!
And you?
Are you a pharmacist now?

Hanna
No!
It's a long story…
What do you sell?

Hannah
Houses!
I've gone up in the world, Hanna.

Hanna
Will I see Nan?

Hannah
Course you will!
She's in a wheelchair now.
Arthritis in her hips.
But she's still sharp,
Still puts it about.

Hanna
Oh it will be wonderful to see her!

Hannah
Nan is beside herself that you're in Margate.

Hanna
I need to find a B&B.

Hannah
You're staying with me, Hanna!

Hanna
Thank you!
You are so kind, so hospitable.
You always were.

Hannah
Steady on!

Hanna
I remember how kind Nan was to us all.

Hannah

Nan's the kind one alright…
Welcome back!
I'll take you round the town.
Jump in.

As Hannah switches on the ignition, 'HELLO'/ADELE is playing.

Hannah drives Hanna around the new Margate.

Hannah

I love a bit of Adele.
Here we go…
The centre of Margate.
Slot machines and shite.
Now it's 'The Old Town'
Everything is vintage
Second-hand clothes and broken lamps –
The more vintage
The better they like it.
You can't buy an orange here.
But people love it.
And look!
There's Dreamland…
Innit beautiful?
It's open again.
Yeah
Margate's changing…at last.

Hanna sings along to the chorus of 'HELLO'.

This is the Turner Gallery.
Weekends
Half of London comes here to see it…
Who'd've thought it, ay?

Margit!

Listening to Hanna singing.

Do you still do a bit of the old karaoke?

Hanna
Sometimes – in the Sports Bar in Pristina.
Me and Sara like it there.
We sing Amy Winehouse, Mylie Cyrus, Adele…

Hannah and Hanna sing the chorus of 'HELLO' together at full blast.

The ice is broken.

18

They get out of the car.

Hannah
Would you like a drink, Hanna?
Before we go to Nan's?
Looking over the beach?

Hanna
Can I smoke here?

Hannah
Out here you can.

Hanna rolls a cigarette

Hannah
I'm having a glass of wine to celebrate!
You?

Hanna
I prefer coffee.

Hannah
How do you take it?

Hanna
Black.

Hannah
You don't drink?

Hanna
No.
I just smoke a lot of cigarettes.

They stand at a bar overlooking the sea.

Hannah drinks white wine.

Hanna lights up.

Pristina has changed too.

Hannah
Oh has it?
Tell me about it...

Hanna
Who are those people at the conference?

Hannah
It's UKIP.
Margate's going up in the world, Hanna.
We've moved on a bit from the days of the National Front...

Hanna
UK Independence Party, right?
Mr Farage!

Hannah
Very knowledgeable!

They're not like the other parties who don't know what they bloody want.

Hanna

There was a man in there who said that the UK should only take Christians from Syria and not Muslims.

Hannah

Well, you can't allow everyone in, can you?

Hanna

I'm a Muslim, Hannah.
Didn't you know?

Hannah

How was I supposed to know that?
It's like asking me to know what colour knickers you're wearing.
He was just trying to make sense of who stays *in* and who stays *out*.
He's not talking about people like you.

Hanna

He *is* talking about people like me.
Even though I am not a practicing Muslim.

Hannah

Don't take it personally.
There are so many refugees now, what can we do?

Hanna

Britain let me and my mother and my brother stay here.
I will never stop being grateful for that.

Hannah

In your day it was just the Kosovans.
They're coming at us from all sides now.
That's what's so difficult.

Hanna
Last time I saw you we were in Kosovo…

Hannah
Of course

Hanna
Have you forgotten?

Hannah
No. Course not.

Pause between them.

Strains of 'AT THE RIVER'/GROOVE ARMADA.

Hanna
It's good to sing again.
With you I mean…

Hannah
Who's Sara?

Hanna
My partner.
We have a flat for four years.

Hannah
She's a woman?

Hanna
Yes.
Sara is a woman.

Hannah
So you're *gay*…

Hanna
Yes
It took me a long time to know that about myself.

Hannah

You're a lesbian?

Hanna

So?

Does that shock you?

Hannah

Sorry.

Bit of a surprise that's all.

You're like…married together?

Hanna

Yes – but in my stupid country you can get beaten up for this.

Not like here where everybody accepts gay people

Where you can have a civil partnership.

Where you can travel anywhere.

In Kosovo we are not even part of the European Union!

And we are in the middle of Europe!

In England you are so *lucky!*

Hannah

Right, you're right.

Hanna

I am so envious of you living in a free country.

Hannah

Depends what you mean by free.

It can't be free to everybody.

Not anymore

Not like in your day Hanna when we welcomed everyone.

The Kosovans who came to Margate in '99…

They've all left now.

It was getting silly.

People weren't having it.

Thank goodness – sorry to say this to you of all people, Hanna –

Thank goodness we put up the drawbridge before this summer.

Look at Calais!

Hanna

What's a drawbridge?

Hannah

It's the only way into a castle.

When it's up

You're out!

And there's no getting in!

Hannah's phone rings.

Hannah

Excuse me, Hanna –

Hanna takes the opportunity to make a call on her phone.

Hannah *(on phone)*

Phelps and Phelps, Hannah speaking...

Hullo, Mrs Hall – as I was saying earlier – it has four bedrooms, all facing the sea, with a double balcony on the master – yes, as Turner would have seen it!

Hanna *(on phone)*

Hullo Albin!

So – Mira?

Oh God!

Nothing?

Hannah *(on phone)*

...almost all original features are intact behind the stud walls and the plyboarding – the marvellous thing is that multi-occupancy has so often *protected* these glorious buildings...

Hanna *(on phone)*
She sings songs!
For UKIP!

Hanna mimics Hannah.

'Illegal immigrants in every town
Stand up and be counted Blair and Brown'
Yes!
That's *Hannah!*

Hannah *(on phone)*
...and when all the additions are in the skip, lo and
behold, an early nineteenth century townhouse emerges in
all its former glory...

Hanna *(on phone)*
Mira's *still* there?

Hannah *(on phone)*
It's a beauty Mrs Hall.
A treat to the eye.

Hanna *(on phone)*
I don't know what to do!
What if Mira comes to Margate – and I'm not here?

Hannah *(on phone)*
Thursday at four-thirty?
Yes, I'll meet you at the property.
Goodbye!

Hanna *(on phone)*
She's coming
I've got to go, got to go...

Both returning to the bar.

Hannah

Sorry.

That was Mrs Hall.

I've sold her one house already…

Hanna

I have a young friend who is in trouble, Hannah.

That is why I have come here.

To Margate, to see you…

Hannah

Sorry? What?

Hanna

Her name is Mira and she is from Syria.

And now she's stuck in Calais.

She needs me.

Hannah

Bloody hell, Hanna, the people there are totally illegal!

They come in any way they can.

Nothing will stop them.

Hanna

That is because they are completely desperate.

They have nowhere to go.

Can I tell you about her?

Hannah

Go on…

Hanna

Three months ago, she arrives in Emergency.

She's from Aleppo.

She'd travelled alone in a lorry from Turkey.

She thought she was on her way to Macedonia but she was wrong.

The driver left her in Pristina.

She didn't know where she was.

She hadn't eaten properly for days.

She had a terrible cough from sleeping out.

And she had nowhere to go.

So she came to live with me and Sara for a month.

We both love Mira.

We have no plans for children but...

Mira is like our child.

Her health improved and her English too.

She told us her story – eventually.

Her family lost their neighbours to a barrel bomb attack.

During the funeral there is *another* barrel bomb attack.

Everyone is killed.

She loses her mother, her father and her two sisters.

She loses her whole family in one day.

But Mira is unharmed.

She is safe.

I want Mira to remain safe.

But how can she stay with us?

What can Kosovo offer her?

Yes, we are independent.

There are nice cafés –

But nothing really changes...

And there is no work!

I offered to get her to my brother Albin in Vienna,

That is the nearest place, the safest place, to claim asylum.

This summer they are welcoming refugees!

They cheer them as they cross the border!

It's true!

I said to Mira, 'You must go there.'
She agreed though she didn't want to leave us.
Then she asked me to tell her *my* story…

Hannah

What's this got to do with me, Hanna?

Hanna

So I told her all about you and about Margate
About the way you followed me to Kosovo…
Talking to Mira made everything come back to me.
I told her about what happened to me in the war –
The courage I felt from you when I came back to Pristina.
The courage not to be ashamed.
She was so moved by my story.
She said that *she* wanted to go to Margate.
To meet you and Nan.
I said,
'When you have your papers – you can go anywhere you like!'
Together Sara and I find the money for her to leave.
Everyone helped.
They are all touched by Mira once they meet her.
Two days after she left me,
Albin is waiting for her at the Austrian border.
He and his family take her into their home.
Like us, they love her.
But…
A week later,
Albin calls to say she's not in her bed this morning.
She left a note to say she's not staying in Vienna.
She's sorry but she doesn't like Austria.
She's going on alone.

To England.
To Margate.

Hannah
To Margate?

Hanna
To you.
To you and Nan.
To your flat.

Hannah
Is this a joke?

Hanna
Not at all.
You are the only people that I know in the UK.
I think you are wonderful.
I just thought you and Nan would do something to help an asylum-seeker.
You helped me!

Hannah
I'm sorry Hanna.
There is no way I can help you.
You're my one and only asylum-seeker.
The last time I helped you out,
All I got was grief.
I'm still paying for it now.

Hanna
Mira is alone and very frightened.

Hannah
Don't talk to me about asylum-seekers, I had my fill.
It's enough to look after myself and my Nan.

It's always others who get the benefits in this country,
Not the people *born* here.
We're going to see Nan.
Can we drop this one?
Now?

19

Hannah rings the buzzer of Nan's flat like she did in the first half.

Hannah *(to intercom, gentler in tone)*
Hi Nan – it's me.
No I've got my key.
I'm bringing a visitor up, OK?
Yes a very special visitor…
All the way from Kosovo!

Hannah *(to Hanna)*
Nan is very excited that you're coming.

Hanna
I'm excited too.

(to audience)
The lift is very small.
Everything is coming back to me.
How will I feel?

Hannah
Nan wheels straight for Hanna.
She's put her Jeremy Corbyn T-shirt on
And her Gay Pride trainers.
Hanna just stands there smiling.

Hanna
I am so happy to see you again!

Hannah

Nan's in tears.

Hanna and Nan reunite

So is Hanna!
The doorbell goes.

Hannah *(as Nan)*

'That'll be Joe – he takes me to the shops once a week –
Wait till he sees you, Hanna!'

Hanna

Joe fills the doorway
So smart in his uniform.

Hannah *(as Nan)*

'He is an Inspector now!'

Hanna

Joe hugs me like a bear.
It's wonderful.

Hannah

Nan's got a tray of biscuits and cake on her wheelchair.

Hannah *(as Nan)*

'Come on now – you all sit down.
Joe – would you be mum?'

Hanna

Joe pours the tea.
'What brings you here, Hanna, after all these years?'

Hannah

I had to speak up;
'Hanna's invited a refugee to live with us.'

Hanna *(to Nan)*

I'm sorry.

I didn't invite her…

I just told her about you all.

Hannah

Nan's face lights up.

'That's wonderful!

Has she got a family?

Bring them too!'

For a moment, everyone lost for words.

Hanna *(to inform Joe and Nan)*

Her name is Mira.

She is fifteen.

She is from Aleppo in Syria.

She's lost her mother and father and both her sisters.

Hannah *(as Nan)*

'Then Mira can stay with me for as long as she likes.'

Hanna

Joe clears his throat;

Hanna *(as Joe)*

'Nan you can't do that, you know.'

Hannah *(as Nan)*

'Why can't I?'

Hanna *(as Joe)*

'She's an unaccompanied child, Nan.

She'd have to go to Dover for screening,

Then to Social Services.'

Hannah *(as Nan)*

'She doesn't have to do that!'

Hanna *(as Joe)*
'They'll put her in foster care.
She has to be with a trained foster parent.'

Hannah *(as Nan)*
'I can be the foster parent.'

Hanna *(as Joe)*
'Nan – it takes six months to train!'

Hannah *(as Nan)*
'I can train!'

Hanna *(as Joe)*
'You're eighty-eight years old!
I'm sorry, Nan…
They'll give her a warrant to go to Croydon and register –
claim asylum.'

Hannah *(as Nan)*
'Croydon?'

Hanna *(as Joe)*
'Has to be Croydon.'

Hannah *(as Nan)*
'And then she can come back to Margate?'

Hanna *(as Joe)*
'No Nan.
There are so many asylum-seekers in Kent!
They can't all stay here.'

Hannah *(as Nan)*
'Where's she going to end up then?'

Hanna *(as Joe)*
'Could be anywhere
Barnsley, Stockton, Coventry…'

Hannah *(as Nan)*

'Coventry!

That is typical of a bloody Tory government!

I'd like to give that Home Secretary woman a piece of my mind!

Pushing a poor girl around like that.'

Hanna *(as Joe)*

'The law's the law, Nan.'

Hannah *(as Nan)*

'Why can't we keep her here?'

Hanna *(as Joe to Hannah)*

'Cos I'd have to put you under arrest.'

Beat.

Hannah *(as Nan)*

'P'raps you better go, Joe.

Us girls have a bit of talking to do.'

Hanna *(as Joe)*

'Look, Nan –'

Hannah *(as Nan with force)*

'I'm sure you are required at an important meeting, Joe!'

Hanna *(to audience)*

Joe leaves.

Hannah *(to audience)*

One hell of a row broke out after he left.

Nan saying how bloody mean our country was to let in only 300 child refugees

and me saying we can't let the lot in can we?

Who's going to pay for thousands of them?

Then Nan telling me I'm a selfish cow.

If I'd lived through a war I wouldn't be so ignorant!
Didn't I understand that the cause of the next holocaust
Would be mean-spirited nimbys like me?
All this was starting to do my head in.

Hanna

I'm sorry, Hannah.
I am still living in the year 2000!

Hannah

Nan and Joe and I got along fine until you turned up!
How much longer are you staying on for your holiday?

Hanna

Don't worry.
I'm going.

Hannah

Sorry it couldn't be longer.

Hanna

Yes, that's too bad!

Hannah

Where are you going?

Hanna

Calais.

Hannah

Calais!
You're mad, you know that don't you?

Hanna

I have to find her.
Austria will not let Mira back in.

Hannah

So what are you going to do with her?

Hanna

Stop her coming to a country which is full of people like you!
Only your Nan understands.
And, like Joe says,
What can she do?
You're the same as you were when I first met you,
You haven't changed a bit!
You think UKIP is better than the National Front?
It's the same party, only they're dressed in a suit and tie.
Can't you see that?
Oh you make me so sad…

(to Nan)
Goodbye Nan.
It was very good to see you.
I wish that my mother could be here too.
I kiss you.

Hannah *(as Nan)*
'Goodbye, Hanna.'

Hanna leaves without a backward look at Hannah.

'If you let that Hanna go,
I'll never forgive you
For as long as I live.

Pause.

And this time
Don't forget your fucking passport!'

20

Soundtrack through.

Hannah runs to a drawer and puts her passport in her bag and runs out of the door.

Hannah kicks off her heels and carries them as she runs along the Margate seafront to the station and onto the platform where Hanna is already on the train.

Hannah boards the train and sits opposite Hanna.

Hannah is totally out of breath.

Soundtrack continues...

Hannah
Are you really going to the Jungle?

Hanna
Dover then Calais.
I've told you
Mira is hiding there and she needs help.

Hannah
Don't do this Hanna.
Just take it easy.
Let's talk.

Hanna
We've talked.
We didn't get anywhere.

Hannah
Calais is a dangerous place.
It's called the Jungle,
It's full of scum.

Traffickers, smugglers, people who'll slit your throat soon
as they look at you.
There's no water, no toilets, the police hate the migrants
and everyone who tries to help them.
It's a human sewer.

Hanna
How do you know?

Hannah
I read it in the *Daily Mail.*

Hanna
Mira is there.
She is on her own.
I am frightened for her,
Not for myself.

Hannah
Look Hanna.
Like I say,
I can't help you this time.
I would do if I could –
But I just do not get how you expect
Ordinary working people
To throw their arms open to these migrants!

Hanna hands Hannah a small blue envelope.

Hannah
What's this?

Hanna
It's the letter you wrote me when you got back to Margate.
Sixteen years ago.

Hannah
Oh…
What did I say?

Voiceover of the sixteen-year-old Hannah.

'Dear Hanna, I'm not good at writing or letters. But what you told me out by that coach has made me cry and cry. I ain't never cried so much before. It's terrible what they did to you. I'm sorry for the times I was cruel to you. You are always welcome in my home. That's a promise. Nan says to give you her best regards because she misses you and your mum and Albin. So do I. I won't never forget you Hanna,
Faithfully yours
Hannah'

Hannah
Did I write that?

Hanna
You did – I know it by heart.

Hannah stares out of the window.

Hannah
What's her name again?

Hanna
Mira!

Hanna finishes the conversation by looking out of the window.

The sound of the train takes over again.

Hannah
What can I do?

Hanna turns and smiles at her.

Hanna
Be my friend.

21

Soundtrack – 'FUCKIN' PERFECT'/P!NK.

In a pop video style, a sustained 'silent' sequence through first sixty-five seconds of song.

Hannah and Hanna leave the train, get a taxi, go through passport control, customs, on to the ferry at Dover; on deck Hannah drinks and Hanna smokes; they disembark and arrive at Calais and go through customs…

Hannah
Security at Calais is something else, barbed wire, dogs, guns, armed patrols.

Hanna
Hannah charms the customs police.

Hannah
Hanna is shaking like we're going into a concentration camp.

Hanna
I am so glad that I am not alone.

Hannah
I don't know what the hell I'm doing here.

Hanna
I don't know where to go.

Hannah
I take a couple of hundred euros out of a wall.
Call a taxi.

(to Hanna)
I can't speak a word of French.

Hanna
Ou se trouve Le Jongle, s'il vous plait?

Hannah
Taxi is going at eighty miles an hour down an auto-route.

Hanna
Taxi stops in the middle of a kind of desert.

Hannah
Sixty euros to nowhere.

Hanna
Wind sand rubbish blowing all over.

Hannah
We look through a big hole in a long fence.

Hanna
I think this is the Jungle.
I can see people moving about.

Hannah
Hanna just walks in.
All her fear has gone.

Hanna walks up to people at random.

Hanna
Have you seen a girl aged fifteen called Mira?

Hannah
Hanna asks everyone in sight, showing them her picture.

Hanna
Everyone shakes their head.

Hannah
They look sorry for Hanna.
I have come in the stupidest clothes for a jungle trip.
The wind here is like a gale that never stops.
It just comes straight off the sea.
And now it's getting dark...

Hanna
The ground is moving!

Hannah
That's not the ground, girl.
That's rats...

Hanna
Rats everywhere!

Hannah
Oh my gawd!
It's disgusting!
How can people *live* here?

Hanna points.

There's a group of men we can ask about Mira

Hannah
Where?

Hanna
Sitting around that fire.

Hannah
Be careful, Hanna! They're all from – well – I don't know
where they're from!

Hanna
Hello can we join you?

Hanna sits down cross-legged with a group of African men
around a small open fire.

I am from Kosovo.
My friend is from England.

Hannah

They all turn on *me,*
Smiling and talking all at once –
'Oh I love England,
I love BBC, the Queen,
Manchester United.
I am going to London.
Every night I try…
Look!
I break my leg on Eurostar!'
I say to them
'How do you know you love it?
You ain't never been there!'

Hanna

They are burning some sticks inside some stones
In the cooking pot.
They have onions.
Only onions.
These young men are from Sudan
Very proud people.

Hannah

They have tents made of plastic flapping in the gale.
No gloves no scarves.

Hanna

They've been here for six months.

Hannah

How can they stand it out here?

Hanna

They offer us onions.
I tell them about Mira.
That she is from Syria –
Where in the Jungle are Syrian people?

Hannah

The Afghans are over there.
The Somalians are on the other side.

Hanna

But where are the Syrians?

Hannah

They don't know.

Hanna

One of the Sudan guys comes running up to us.
'The Syrians! They are not here!
They are in Calais.
By the harbour
Not out here in the Jungle.'

Hannah

We leave the Jungle.
Hit the road.
It's night now and it's cold.
A few cars, no taxis
We walk towards the lights in the far distance.
Back to Calais

Hannah and Hanna walk together along the endless road back to the centre of Calais.

What do you do, Hanna?

Hanna

I'm an ambulance driver.

Hannah

Oh

Quite dangerous

Putting your life at risk and that…

Do you get any perks like, you know, holidays or anything?

Hanna

No, no, I haven't gone on holiday for fifteen years,

The last time I went on holiday I was in Margate….

This time I've used up all my savings to get here.

Hannah

Oh I'm sorry.

Hanna

Do you go on holidays?

Hannah

Oh yeah, you know, couple of times a year,

Spain, mostly…

Hanna

What do you do?

Hannah

Lie on the beach.

Get a tan…

Have a laugh.

Hanna

And do you have a partner?

Hannah

Um well yeh there's someone.

It's complicated.

Hanna

Oh.

Is he married?

Hannah

Technically.

But, yeah, its over.

He just hasn't told her yet.

Hanna

Ah ha, OK.

So he's a man.

Hannah

Well yeah, I'm not a lesbian.

Hanna

No no I didn't think you were.

So do you like him?

Are you in love with him?

Hannah

Steve?

Yeah, Steve.

He loves me.

He says.

But no I wouldn't say I was in love with him exactly.

Hanna

OK...

Hannah

Kosovan men are quite handsome, you know.

Your brother Albin is quite a looker.

Hanna

Well yes, and Kosovan women are very beautiful too!

I don't know why…
I've never understood the attraction of men
That's what I'm trying to say

Hannah
You've got a point there

Hanna
Those men from Sudan were beautiful Hannah.
Each one of them.

Hannah
I wouldn't go that far.

Hanna
So kind to us.
So noble.
They offered us their food.

Hannah
Yuk!

Hanna
They've come 3000 miles from Sudan.
Civil war, genocide and starvation.
And they offer us food.

Hannah
Why would anyone in their right mind sit in a dustbin bag,
eating onions, outdoors in a perishing wind off the North
Sea, hoping to break into a country that doesn't want them?

Hanna
It's simple.
No one wants them.
And they believe in England Hannah.
They really believe in your country.

To them it's the last place of values and decency,
A country where everyone has a chance to begin again.
A country that is not racist.
You just have no idea what your nation means to everyone,
To everyone who is lost in the world...
Look – a bus!

Hannah
We jump on the bus.
I pay the driver.

Hanna
The Sudanese are on too.

Hannah *(to Hanna)*
We are the only white people on this bus.

Hanna
Do you want to get off?

Hannah
I'm just *saying,* Hanna!

Hanna
The Sudanese are going out to the auto-route to jump lorries
Like they are going to battle!
They are wonderful!

Hanna throws kisses at them as she gets off the bus.

Good luck!
In Pristina I will remember you!

Hannah
We are standing by a disused warehouse.
It's dark and it's starting to rain on us.

Hanna

The Syrians must be somewhere near to here.

Hannah

Can't we find them in the morning?
Get a bit of sleep first?
Come on Hanna.

Hanna

No.

Hannah

I can afford a hotel for the two of us.
Just *accept* it Hanna.
Let me treat you!

Hanna

I will never find Mira by staying in a hotel

Hannah

You are totally chronic!
Mother Hanna fucking Teresa, that's you.

Hanna

Hannah – look!

Hannah

We come around the corner and…
There's a dozen people sleeping in this big church doorway.
Sleeping bags up close to each other.
Big sign over their heads
'SYRIA'.
They got cooking things like when you go camping.
Big laundry bags with all their stuff in.
And there's a giant in a woolly hat and five fleeces
Making coffee
It smells great…

Hanna

Have you seen this girl?
She is from Aleppo
Her name is Mira
She is in Calais
I am looking for her
Please can you help me?

Hannah

Everyone looks.
They seriously look
One by one.
Each man shakes his head
And hands back the picture
Very respectful.
One points up the street
Giving her directions.
Hanna turns to me to follow her
As I turn
The giant making the coffee
He smiles at me
Gestures
Holds out a cup.
Y'know what?
I smiled back.
Walked straight up
Took the cup
And drank a bullet of sweet black coffee in one shot.

Strains of 'FUCKIN' PERFECT'/P!NK.

Round the corner…
And there's another dozen guys!
Same set-up

They're on a ramp of an old loading bay.
They've got an open-air kitchen.
An old man is cutting bread.
Young men are smoking,
Watching us…

Hanna

Have you seen this girl?
She is from Aleppo.
Her name is Mira.
She is in Calais.
I am looking for her.
Please can you help me?

Hannah

It all goes the same way.
They look.
They shake their heads.
Then the old man limps across to a shutter
at the end of the loading bay.
He raises it up this high.
All I can see is darkness.
Out of the darkness walks a tall young woman in a headscarf.
She has a tiny baby in her arms.
She goes over to Hanna and asks to see the picture
She looks at it closely.
She says, 'Mira.'

Hanna

Mira?
You know her?
The woman looks at me closely.
'You are Hanna?'
'I am Hanna'

She reaches out her free hand and touches mine
'Mira talked about you all the time.
She has lost her family.'
I say
'Yes…
Thank you…
Where is she!?'
She looks very closely at me again
'She's gone.
She is on auto-route now.
Everybody on auto-route now.
Fighting
Very dangerous for young girl.'
Fighting?
'Yes
Everyone is fighting.
Fighting for lorry.'

Hannah

Then the woman with the child steps forward and takes a
card from her pocket.

She hands Hanna a postcard.

Hanna

'This is from Mira to you.'
Thank you. Thank you. Thank you.

Hannah

They shake our hands.
They close the shutter
and they're gone.

Hanna reads the postcard from Mira.

Hanna

'Dear Hanna –

Now I go to England.

England is free.

Albin was very kind to me but I felt a stranger.

I remember all you said about England.

If I live I will walk to Margate.

Find Hannah and Nan.

Thank you thank you thank you a thousand times.

Mira xxxx'

I *told* her never to go alone.

Pause.

Hannah

Look what you've done.

Your fairy story about England has risked this girl's life!

She should have stayed in Austria with your brother!

And *if* she survives

I'm the one who's meant to take her in!

Don't look at me!

I can't help her!

22

Hanna starts walking fast, she is looking inside car windows.

Hannah

Where're you going?

What you doing?

Hanna

I don't need your help

You go to a hotel!

Hannah

You can't just dump me you know.
Not here.
Not when I've actually come here to help you!
Like you *asked* me to.
You just won't admit you're in the wrong!
And you are Hanna!

Hanna stops by an old van.

She won't be in there you know.
Just give up Hanna!

Hanna opens the door of an old van, gets in.

Hanna!
What do you think you're doing?
This is not your van!

Hanna starts the engine by connecting the wires of the ignition, Hanna is a skilled ambulance driver and knows how to drive fast in traffic.

Hanna

Have you got sat nav on your phone?

Hannah

Yes.
What are you doing Hanna?
How did you start it?
You can't steal someone's van!

Hanna starts the van and they are off at high speed.

I haven't put my seatbelt on yet!

Hanna

We must find Mira!

Calm down.
I do this every day.
Which way to the A16?
She'll be at the lorry park.

Hannah
I'm not doing this.

Hanna *(shouts)*
WHICH WAY TO THE A16?

Hannah
Alright Hanna!

The female sat nav voice speaks:

'In 200 yards do a U-turn
In 200 yards do a U-turn'

Soundscape.

Hannah and Hanna travel at speed, according to Hannah's sat nav, towards the part of the auto-route where Hanna might find Mira trying to board a lorry.

Hanna
Friday morning in Calais.

Hannah
Rush hour madness.

Hanna
Three lanes of traffic leaving France.

Hannah
Three lanes of traffic coming into France.

Hanna
The auto-route is packed.

Hannah

Coaches, caravans, family cars on an overnight.

Hanna

And lorries…

Hannah

A thousand lorries crawling to the port in the slow lane.

Hanna

A long slow line that stretches out as far as I can see.

Hannah

Far away on the *other* side of the auto-route,
A pack of youths watch the lorries

Hanna

Somalians Afghans Sudanese Syrians

Hannah

Pointing, shouting, screaming, pushing –
They all believe they'll be in England tomorrow.

Hanna

Who's going to be the first out of the Jungle?
Who dares?

Hannah

They stampede across the auto-route like wild horses.

Sound of mass honking of horns and cars braking at speed.

Hanna

Look!

Hannah

They're insane!

Hanna

How many?

Hannah

Twenty!?

Hanna

All young guys?

Hannah

Think so.

Hanna

Can you see a girl?

Hannah

All I can see are maniacs!
Take it easy Hanna!
Oh my God!
You almost ran that one over!

Screech of tyres

Hannah

She can't be out here.
It's mayhem and murder.

Hanna

Mira is on the A16.
We have to get to the entrance to the lorry park.
That's where she'll be.

Hannah

Hanna's doing eighty.
Outside lane.
She's swerving past the maniacs.
I look ahead.
'Look Hanna, you're going to miss the exit to the lorry park!'

Screeching of tyres, protesting horns.

She checks the mirror.

Does a right angle across three lanes.

And we're on the slip road!

At eighty miles an hour!

I am having a heart attack.

We are going to fly over the barrier.

But we don't.

She slows the van.

G-force in my guts.

My stomach churns.

She stops.

I open my eyes…

I throw up out the window.

Hanna stops the van and jumps out.

Hanna
I'll be back!

Hannah
You can't just leave me in your stolen van Hanna!

Hanna
Then come with me!
Mira will be here.

Soundscape of near-riot outside closed windows of the van.

Hannah
There's a HUGE gang of men out there!
They are fighting to get in each lorry that passes!
I am not getting out!

Hanna
Please, Hannah, I need you.

Hannah

There's a guy slitting the canvas with a box-cutter.

They're carrying knives Hanna!

Hanna

OK! See you soon!

Hannah gets out of the van.

Hannah and Hanna walk into a melee of young men shouting, lorries starting and traffic passing on the other side of the barrier.

Hannah

We walk into the mob.

There's way more than twenty.

Hundreds more like,

All in a fever, trying to board lorries.

Nearly all blokes,

Mostly young…

There's a woman with a little boy…

As far as I can see,

Both of them don't stand a chance.

Hanna *(to many people)*

Have you seen this girl?

She is from Aleppo,

Her name is Mira.

She is in Calais.

I am looking for her.

Please can you help me?

Hannah

We walk up and down the lorries.

Past the gendarmes who do nothing to stop anyone.

Past drivers locked in their cabins…

Hanna

I can't see her anywhere.

Hannah

Maybe she's hiding in a lorry?

Hanna *(at top of her voice)*
Mira! Mira!
I can't see her
Oh Mira…

Hanna cries tears of frustration.

She *is* alive.
Mira *will* be alright.

Hannah

If she's here Hanna,
I know you'll find her.

Hanna *(tearful)*
I will I will I will I will I will

Hannah comforts Hanna.

Hanna *(practical)*
Ok, let's take back the van.

Hannah

Yeah, let's do that.
We don't want to be arrested.
And I've got an appointment with Mrs Hall tomorrow.

*Hannah and Hanna sing the first verse and chorus of 'FUCKIN'
PERFECT'/P!NK.*

*They sing this without any contact between each other but in
perfect unison.*

23

Soundscape changes.

Hannah

We drive back quite slowly.
Hanna looks for Mira all the way.
She takes the van back to the same street
From which she stole it.
Let's get moving Hanna before the owner comes back.

Hanna

No – I'll take you to the ferry port.
Then I've got to find Mira.
I'm going back on the auto-route.

Hannah

It's not safe there, Hanna!

Hanna

That's where she is most likely to be.

Hannah

She *might* be on the boat to Dover!

Hanna

I hope not.
If I find her,
I'm going to pull her off the lorry.
I'm not bringing her to England.
I want to take her home.

Hannah

To *Kosovo?*

Hanna

Yes

Hannah

Apply for asylum in *Kosovo?*

Hanna

Why not?

I see Kosovo differently now.

You heard Joe.

England is a detention centre.

How will she be treated?

No better than a prisoner.

No one wants her.

Who will care about her?

In Kosovo, at least she will have me and Sara.

We'll make a home for her.

It's all my fault.

I told her a stupid fairytale –

A fairytale about a country that doesn't exist anymore.

And a friend that I pretended I still had

When I knew she had forgotten me long ago.

If Mira's still here,

She's coming home with me.

(to Hannah, with force)

Please – go!

I must go back to the auto-route

Hannah

You're crazy.

You'll be arrested.

Hannah's phone rings.

Bloody hell!

That'll be Mrs Hall

Sorry, Hanna…

Into phone.

Phelps and Phelps, Hannah speaking…
Hullo Mrs Hall –
Oh Nan it's *you!*
Oh…
What do you mean you want to speak to Hanna?
Alright Alright!
I'll put you on loudspeaker
I am hurrying!

Hannah puts her phone onto loudspeaker.

Nan's (pre-recorded) voice comes out loud and clear.

Voiceover of Nan
Hullo Hanna
I'm so glad that my Hannah found you
We couldn't let you go just like that could we?
I'd never forgive myself if you didn't feel welcome here in
Margate.
After fifteen years!
Well Hanna.
I've got some very good news for you –
Mira has arrived!

Hanna
Oh my God (Oh Zoti im)

Voiceover of Nan
Mira's safe and well here with me.
Somehow or other she got to Dover,
Then walked twenty-two miles to Margate.
She's had a bath.
I've fed her.
She's sitting here in my chair,

in Hannah's old dressing gown.

She's so young and I think she's very brave.

She's safe, Hanna.

And I'm not telling Joe about her neither!

Hanna

Oh Nan!

How is she?!

Voiceover of Nan *(to Mira)*

Mira!

Come over here!

Voiceover of Nan *(to Hanna)*

I'll put her on

Voiceover of Mira *(very young, slow, fragile, a voice that we haven't heard before)*

Hullo

I'm so happy to be here.

Nan is wonderful.

She is so kind to me.

Like I am her daughter,

She make me so welcome.

I love the flat

It feels like…like…

I have a home

Thank you.

Hannah and Hanna

Thank you!

MUSIC

Hannah and Hanna stand there, stunned.

Soundscape and lights fade to…

EPILOGUE/Autumn 2018

Hannah and Hanna put on their 2018 coats.

Hannah
Hanna came back to Margate with me
To welcome Mira.
It was a happy scene.

Hanna
But my visa had almost expired.
I had to go home.

Hannah
I will never forget the look she gave me when she left.
Mira was so happy to be with Nan
You couldn't think of moving her.
She is a lovely girl.
She touched us all.
Yes.
Even me.
The fairy story that Hanna had told Mira about England
turned out to be true.
Nan loved her from the minute she arrived.
Joe taught her to speak up for herself.
And slowly I got to know Mira.
Thanks to Hanna,
Mira saw me as someone perfect.
I tried very hard to change her mind.
I couldn't.
I sometimes wanted just to run away.
I was doing well with Phelps, selling houses, making good
money.

And for once I had a good relationship on the go.

I didn't want to lose my independence.

My freedom.

Then, one night

I dreamt that Mira fell out of the eleventh floor window of our flats.

I woke up in flood of tears.

I couldn't stop even when I woke.

Hanna

She called me in Pristina.

She said that she wanted to look after Mira herself.

To be…

To be her guardian.

Would I be happy with that?

Yes, I said,

Yes yes yes.

Hannah

While we waited to hear about Mira's case,

I trained to be a foster-parent.

Mira and I are like mother and daughter now.

Can you believe it?

I can't imagine life without her.

Hanna

Last year,

The day before her ninetieth birthday,

Nan died.

I went to Margate for the funeral.

Sara came too.

Nan would have been so happy to see us all come together.

Like a family.

I want Mira and Hanna to visit us in Pristina.

Hannah

We want to go too.
Mira's eighteen next month,
And we don't yet know what will happen.
We're waiting to hear if she has leave to remain…

Hanna

To keep our spirits up while we wait
We're singing karaoke together –
On SKYPE!
Mira cringes a bit when we get going –
But sometimes she joins in too…

Hannah and Hanna sing 'HELLO'/ADELE.

As thery sing, an enlarged picture of Mira, the same one that Hanna has used throughout part 2, appears illuminated on the back screen.

THE END

9 781786 826435